Separate Worlds

by Deborah Akers

 HOUGHTON MIFFLIN HARCOURT
School Publishers

PHOTOGRAPHY CREDITS: Cover © Bettmann/CORBIS; tp © Don Cravens/Time & Life Pictures/Getty Images; 4 © Bettmann/CORBIS; 5 © Jack Delano/Library of Congress Prints and Photographs Division Washington, DC 20540s; 6 © Eudora Welty/CORBIS; 7 © Hank Walker/Time Life Pictures/Getty Images; 8 © Associated Press; 9 © Don Cravens/ Time & Life Pictures/Getty Images; 12 © Flip Schulke/CORBIS; 13 © Bettmann/CORBIS; 14 © William Lovelace/Express/ Getty Images

Printed in China

ISBN-13: 978-0-547-02281-9
ISBN-10: 0-547-02281-6

5 6 7 8 0940 18 17 16 15 14 13 12
4500351694

Table of Contents

*I*magine yourself on a hot summer day. What are some things you like to do?

Maybe you dream of getting a nice cold ice cream at a nearby restaurant. Thirsty? How about sipping some ice cold water? If you prefer to stay inside, you might enjoy getting a good seat at the movies.

Segregation was common in the southern part of the United States during the 1950s. Segregation meant that African Americans were set apart from other people. It also meant that you would not get to spend your summer day quite the way you imagined.

Nice Cool Water

When segregation was allowed, there were separate drinking fountains labeled *White* and *Colored*. If your drinking fountain was not working, you were out of luck.

How about going swimming? Only white children could swim in the clean public pool. African American children had to find a different way to stay cool.

African Americans could not drink from the same fountains as white people.

African Americans could not eat at any restaurant they chose.

A Tasty Treat

Are you still in the mood for that ice cream? Here is another example of what it was like to live under segregation. Some restaurants served only white people, and African Americans could not eat there. You would have fewer choices of restaurants to go to for that ice cream, and they might not be close by.

At the Movies

Are you ready to find a great seat at the movies? During the time of segregation, going to the movies might not have been quite as much fun. African Americans had to go through a separate door, and they had to sit apart from white people. They had to sit in a certain section.

African Americans had to sit apart from white people in theaters.

African Americans had to give up their seats on the bus.

Going Places

Do you have a favorite place to sit when you ride on the bus? Under segregation, African Americans did not have many choices about where they wanted to sit on a city bus. They could only sit in the back seats. If a white person wanted their seat, they had to stand up for the rest of the bus ride.

Unfair Times

In the 1950s, the law said that people should be treated "separate but equal." This meant that African Americans had separate restaurants, stores, and schools. These places were supposed to be equal to the ones white people had. However, this was often not the case. There were numerous unfair laws in many states.

African Americans could not use the white waiting rooms.

Rosa Parks would not give up her seat.

A Seat on the Bus

On December 1, 1955, a woman named Rosa Parks got on the city bus in Montgomery, Alabama. She was tired from working all day. Then, a white man got on the bus. He wanted her seat. Rosa Parks said no. She was arrested. Other African Americans were angry after this injustice. Parks' simple action began the Civil Rights Movement in the United States.

African Americans in Montgomery decided to stop riding city buses. Some walked or carpooled to school and work instead. Their action was called a boycott. Because there were fewer passengers, the bus companies started to lose money.

On December 20, 1956, the law changed. African Americans in Montgomery were able to sit in any seat on the bus. The boycott had worked. Most importantly, it was done in a peaceful way.

Key Events During the Montgomery Bus Boycott

1955

December 1, 1955 Rosa Parks is arrested for not giving up her seat on the bus.

December 5, 1955 African Americans walk or carpool to work or school rather than ride the bus.

1956

1956 The Montgomery Bus Boycott continues all year.

December 20, 1956 The law says that African Americans can sit in any seat on buses in Montgomery.

11

The Dream

Martin Luther King, Jr., was one leader of the Montgomery bus boycott. He dreamed of equal rights for all African Americans. Dr. King's speeches captured people's hearts. He believed that people must always act without hurting others. Many African Americans listened to what Dr. King said and tried to stand up for their rights peacefully.

Dr. King encouraged people to resist segregation.

African Americans sat down in restaurants that were only for whites.

Peace in Action

African Americans thought of many other ways to resist segregation. Some would go to restaurants that only served white people. They did not leave even though no one would serve them a nourishing meal. Some even got arrested. Through it all, they tried to recall Dr. King's teachings and were always peaceful and polite.

Many African Americans marched for their rights.

All kinds of people fought for better rights for African Americans, including white people. People marched for voting rights and the right to equal schools. Some people went to jail, and some got hurt in these encounters. But they never gave up. The separate worlds of African Americans and whites were slowly brought together into one.

Responding

✔ **TARGET VOCABULARY** **Word Builder** The letters *in* or *un* at the front of most words mean "not" or "no" as in the word injustice. What other words do you know that start with the word parts *in* or *un*? Copy and complete the chart below.

Word	Meaning
incorrect	not correct
unfair	not fair
?	?
?	?

✎ Write About It

Text to Text What other books have you read where someone was treated unfairly? Write a paragraph describing how that person was treated unfairly and why. Use words from the Word Builder in your description.

✔ **TARGET STRATEGY** **Monitor/Clarify** Notice what is confusing as you read. Find ways to understand it.

Word Teaser What vocabulary word rhymes with what you call a group of people who are working or playing together?